Written by Charis Mather

EDINBURGH

Capitals of the UK

©2024
BookLife Publishing Ltd.
King's Lynn, Norfolk
PE30 4LS, UK

All rights reserved.
Printed in India.

A catalogue record for this book is available from the British Library.

ISBN: 978-1-80505-611-9

Written by:
Charis Mather

Edited by:
Noah Leatherland

Designed by:
Amelia Harris

All facts, statistics, web addresses and URLs in this book were verified as valid and accurate at time of writing. No responsibility for any changes to external websites or references can be accepted by either the author or publisher.

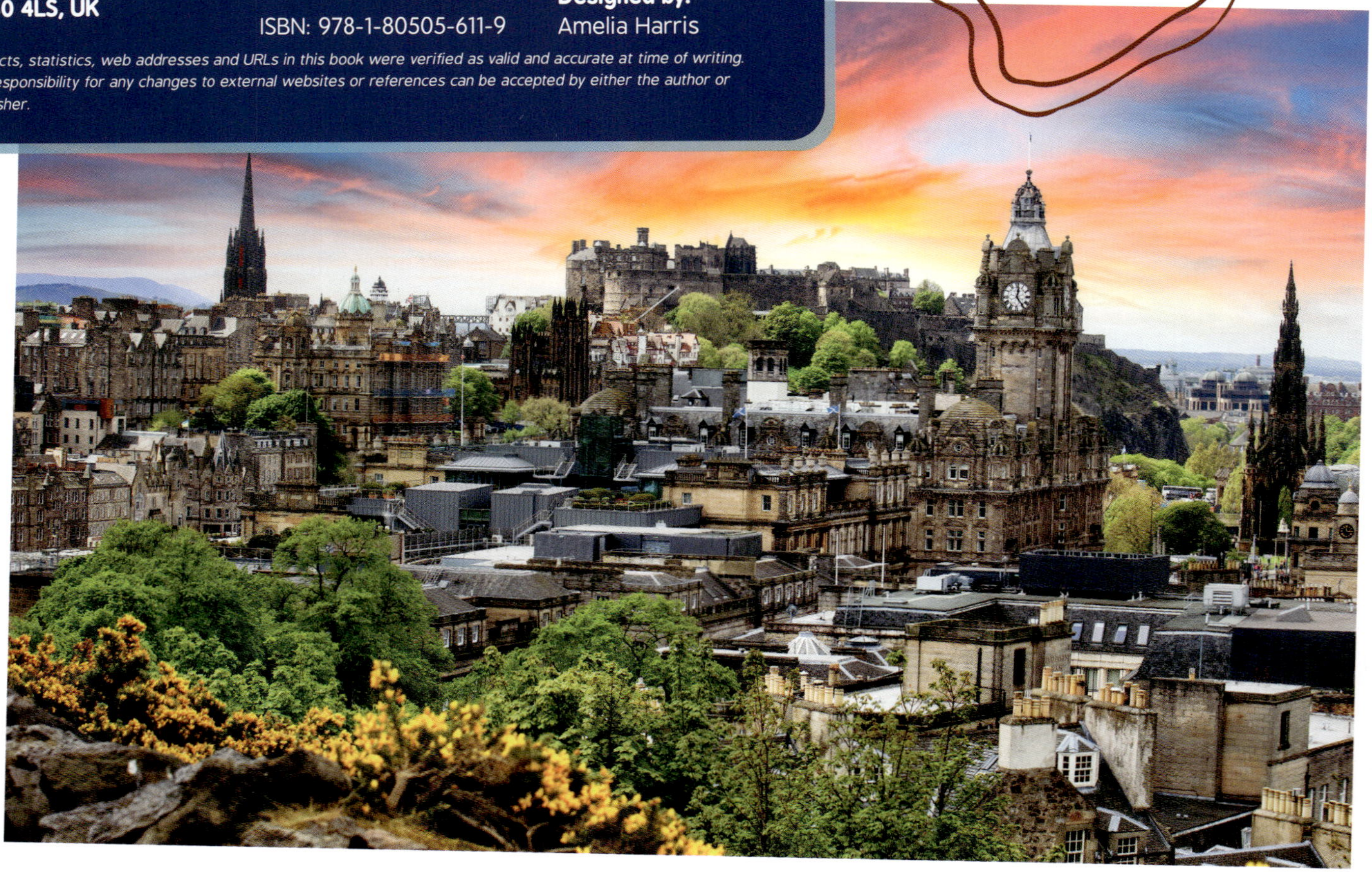

Image Credits

All images are courtesy of Shutterstock.com, unless otherwise specified. With thanks to Getty Images, Thinkstock Photo and iStockphoto. Cover – Perfectorius, anon_tae, Richie Chan, Kamira, Tetiana Dickens, StockImageFactory.com. Recurring images – Voin_Sveta, ArtMari, Mutiah Sari Mustakim, Natasha Pankina, Liliana Danila. 2–3 – Aleks Melnik, TTstudio. 4–5 – Maxger, Leonid Andronov. 6–7 – okili77, Kalinin Ilya, Kamira. 8–9 – anthonycz, MarcAndreLeTourneux, Wenceslas Hollar, Public domain, via Wikimedia Commons. 10–11 – Sasha_Ivv, Aleks Melnik, agsaz, John Slezer, Public domain, via Wikimedia Commons. 12–13 – Gaid Kornsilapa, Nattapoom V, Leonid Andronov. 14–15 – Kit Leong, TTstudio, Kamira, GoodStudio. 16–17 – Angelina Dimitrova, Duirinish Light. 18–19 – Sergii Figurnyi, FCG, Yevgen Kravchenko. 20–21 – David Fitzell, Edinburghcitymom, Marti Bug Catcher. 22–23 – Maxger, Alexey Fedorenko, Prettyawesome, Checco2, Karol Kozlowski.

CONTENTS

Page 4	Welcome to Edinburgh!
Page 6	My Capital, My Country
Page 8	Edinburgh's Early Days
Page 10	Castle City
Page 12	Many a Monument
Page 14	Churches, Kirks and Cathedrals
Page 16	Making Edinburgh Modern
Page 18	Scenic Sights
Page 20	City of Culture
Page 22	Only in Edinburgh
Page 24	Glossary and Index

Words that look like this can be found in the glossary on page 24.

Welcome to Edinburgh!

Edinburgh is my favourite city in the world. This city has hundreds of years of history, so there are plenty of interesting spots to visit and learn about.

The best part about living in Edinburgh is that there are many great places to walk around. I like to bring my camera with me so that I can take pictures of my favourite places.

My Capital, My Country

Like a lot of Scottish cities, Edinburgh is quite hilly.

Edinburgh is the capital city of Scotland. A capital city is often the most important city in a country. Most of the decisions on how to run Scotland are made in Edinburgh.

Scotland is one of four countries that make up the United Kingdom, along with England, Wales and Northern Ireland. Scotland is the farthest north and is often colder than the other countries of the United Kingdom.

Edinburgh's Early Days

Edinburgh first became a capital city in 1437. When the city became crowded a few hundred years later, plans were made to expand. An area called the New Town was added onto the Old Town.

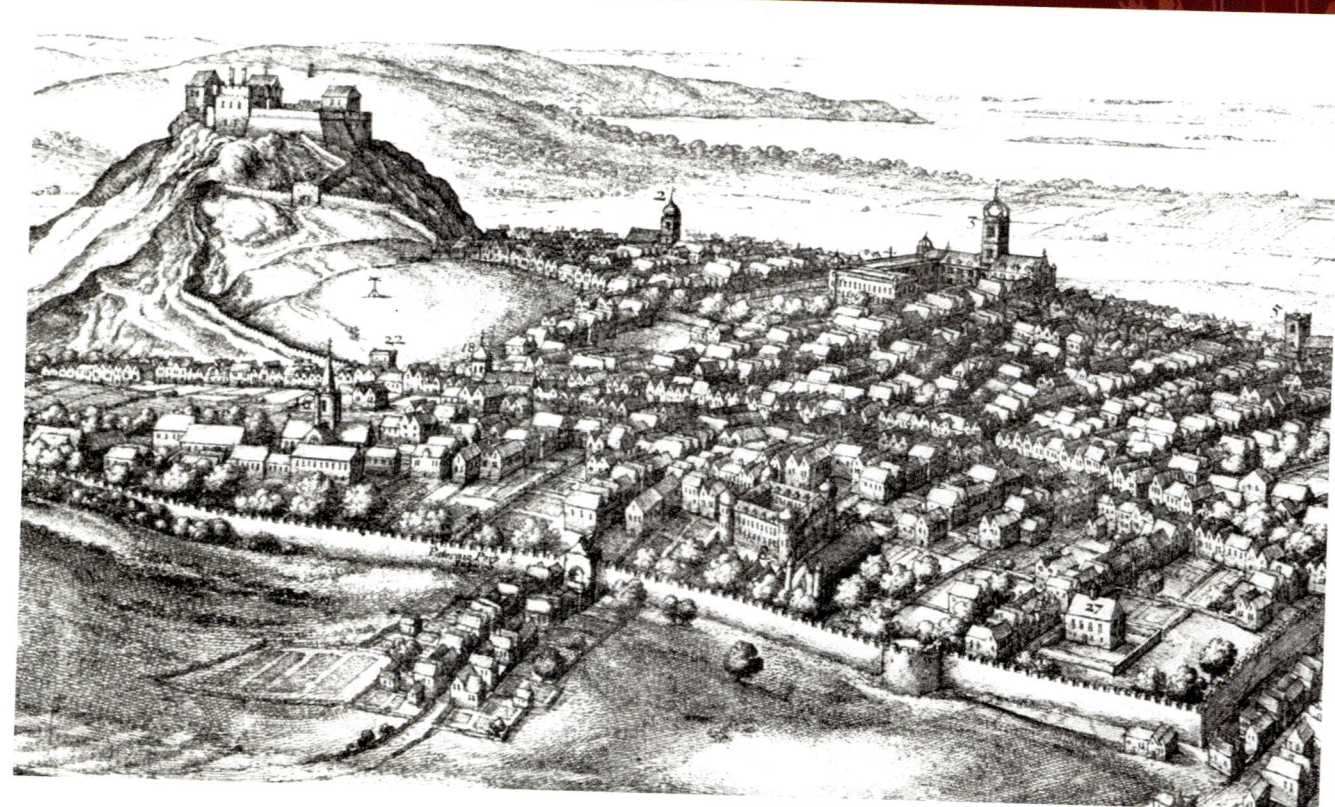

Edinburgh in 1670, before New Town was built

The Old and New Towns are connected by a large bridge, called North Bridge. This bridge does not cross a river, like many bridges do. Instead, North Bridge crosses a set of train tracks.

North Bridge

Castle City

Edinburgh Castle

Edinburgh has a lot of old castles. The most famous castle in this city is Edinburgh Castle. It sits at the top of a rocky hill that overlooks the whole city. The hill was once a <u>volcano</u>.

Edinburgh Castle is over 900 years old. Its high spot up on the hill was a great <u>defence</u> in the past. The castle has stood through many attacks from enemy armies over the years.

Many a Monument

The whole city of Edinburgh is full of historic sites, including many monuments. They are some of the best places to learn about important people and events of the past.

Scott Monument

Some of the main monuments in Edinburgh are on Calton Hill.

The Dugald Stewart Monument

The Nelson Monument was made to look like an upside-down telescope.

The National Monument of Scotland was built to look like a famous building in Greece.

Churches, Kirks and Cathedrals

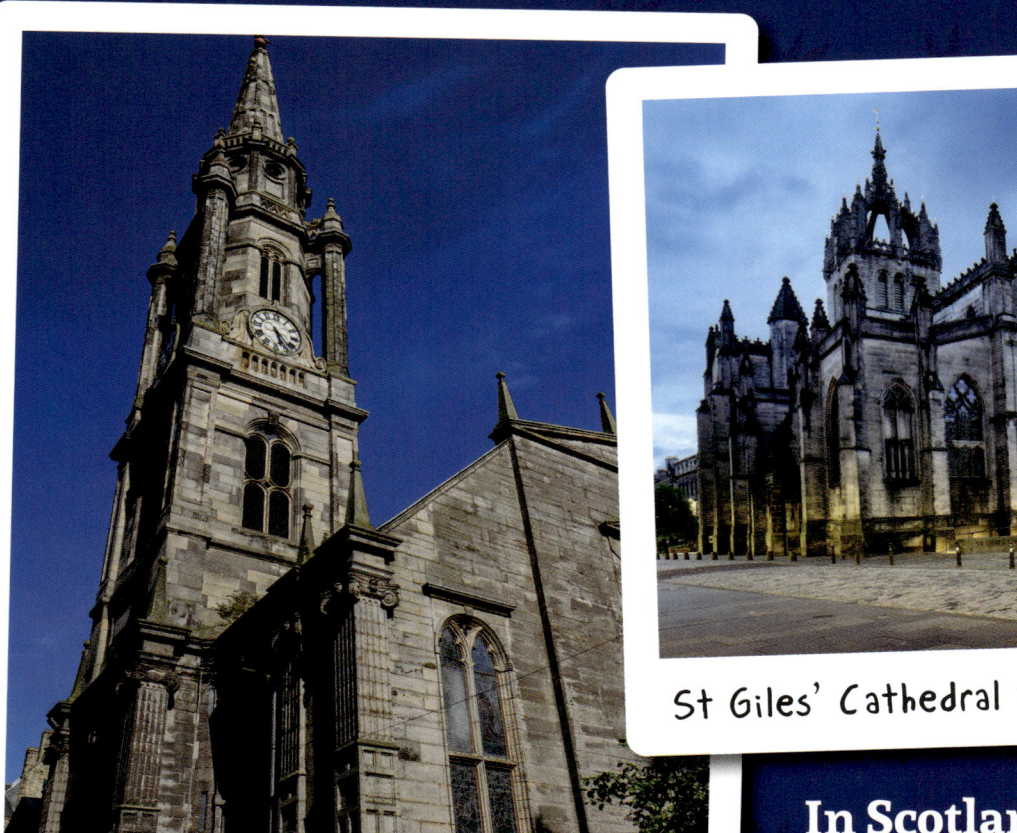

St Giles' Cathedral is around 900 years old.

Tron Kirk is nearly 400 years old, although it is not used as a church now.

In Scotland, churches are sometimes called kirks. You can find some very old and impressive kirks in Edinburgh.

Greyfriars Bobby, near Greyfriars Kirk

There is a statue of Edinburgh's most famous dog, Greyfriars Bobby, near Greyfriars Kirk. When Bobby's owner was buried close to the kirk, Bobby watched over and protected the grave for 14 years.

Making Edinburgh Modern

Not everything in Edinburgh is old. It has some interesting newer structures too. The Scottish Parliament building is <u>modern</u>. Its shape is totally different to any other building in the city.

The Scottish Parliament is where lots of politicians gather to have important meetings. The building's open, glassy design is very different to the stony castles that Edinburgh is famous for.

Scenic Sights

Even though many people come to Edinburgh to see the buildings, there is also a lot of <u>natural</u> beauty to enjoy as well. At Arthur's Seat, you can enjoy looking at both!

Arthur's Seat is a rocky hill with a great view of Edinburgh.

The Water of Leith

The Water of Leith is Edinburgh's main river. It was once very useful for lots of <u>industries</u> that helped Edinburgh grow. Now, the river is an important home to many plants and animals.

City of Culture

One of the best ways to learn about Edinburgh's <u>culture</u> is to experience its events and <u>traditions</u>. Every year, Edinburgh holds a massive festival of art, culture and <u>comedy</u> that celebrates many talented people.

People come from all around the world for the Edinburgh Festival Fringe.

On New Year's Eve, many Scottish people enjoy Hogmanay celebrations.

Hogmanay celebrations usually include fireworks.

In Edinburgh, some people have started a new tradition of dressing up and going to the River Forth for a swim the day after Hogmanay.

Only in Edinburgh

Edinburgh is definitely worth visiting. There is nowhere else like it. I hope you enjoyed seeing some of my favourite spots. When you come, you will have to take photos of your favourite places.

I could tell you about many more exciting places in my home city, but I think you would enjoy discovering them yourself.

The Royal Observatory

Royal Botanic Gardens

Holyrood Palace

What was your favourite place to learn about today?

Glossary

comedy	the art of entertaining in a funny way
culture	the traditions, ideas and ways of life of a group of people
defence	protection, or something that gets in the way of an attack
industries	types of activities and business
modern	to do with recent or present times
natural	to do with nature and things not made by humans
politicians	people who are in charge of making the big decisions in a country
traditions	activities or ways of acting that have been around for a long time
volcano	a mountain that sometimes erupts, giving off very hot melted rock and gases

Index

bridges 9
buildings 13, 16–18
castles 10–11, 17
decisions 6
dogs 15

festivals 20
hills 6, 10–11, 13, 18
rivers 9, 19, 21
views 18